Samuel Sewall Sails for Home

I Rest
your obliged friend
Samuel Sewall.

SAMUEL SEWALL
SAILS FOR HOME

Poetry by
Robert Chute

Coyote Love Press
Portland, Maine 1986

Illustrations are courtesy of the Massachusetts Historical Society.

This chapbook represents the third in the Maine Arts Commission's Annual Chapbook Competition. Copies of this book, as well as the other chapbooks in this series, can be obtained from the Maine Writers and Publishers Alliance, 19d Mason Street, Brunswick, Maine 04011.

To Vicki

FOREWORD

IT'S not trees, rivers, and mountains that make a place, but language and images. I'm thinking of what remains when we close our eyes, how something said and seen two centuries ago continues to be an excellent conduit for the imagination at this latitude. The old diaries are full of such passages. To read them, to linger over certain images and turns of phrase, is to realize their magic properties. All the marvels of the visible and invisible world hinted at. Their victims and actors brought back to life so that they may continue to haunt us.

That's what Robert Chute has done. He has based his sequence of poems on the late seventeenth- and early eighteenth-century diaries of Samuel Sewall. What must have amazed the poet, and what amazes us as readers, aside from other considerations, is the beauty of the writing. There are anecdotes, religious musings, elegies for his dead wife, weather reports, and notations of daily events in the community. What the best entries have in common is conciseness of description, which Chute uses as a model:

> Benjamin Gourd, bound tightly,
> comes to the gallows tree.

If in good poetry less means more, this is a fine example. Like a woodcut in some old tract on Seven Deadly Sins, or some dog-eared, Gothic-lettered page of a cautionary fable—there's no color. Gray and blacks predominate in such writing. The many shades and nuances of blacks and grays.

> Riding down from Newbury just
> at dusk to find black plumes
> smothering all joy of home.

We know the devil lurks behind a tree, spying on the rider. Hell and its torments are close by. The sparks the hooves of the horse make might come from the hellfires below. All the agents of our damnation and salvation are on intimate terms. The stage is small. Each poem in this book is like a puppet theatre stage, and yet all the worldly and otherworldly actors are present. *The Secret Life and Martyrdom of Samuel Sewall* might be the play's title.

Robert Chute's ear and eye for detail, the mastery of his craftsmanship and the intelligence of his choice among the diaries, make this an exemplary work. This is poetry of great clarity, lyric power, and subtlety. The poems summon our imaginations—our own, as well as our ancestral ones. As the poet says here—in another context:

> . . . I write this not
> to upbraid, but only to advise
> you and pray God commands you
> to see the truth and your eyes
> should show you, your heart know, true
> joy in what you would despise.

Let that be the introduction.

CHARLES SIMIC
Juror, Poetry Chapbook
Competition

PREFACE

THIS cycle of 18 poems is based on entries in the diary of Samuel Sewall (1652–1729). The diary entries were begun in December, 1673 and the last was in December, 1729. All except the last, the deathbed poem, draw quite directly from the diary and thus the places, events, and people mentioned, including the Sewalls' many children, are all real.

The edition of the diary available to me was the two-volume set published by Farrar, Straus and Giroux in 1973 and edited by M. Halsey Thomas. The quotations at the head of each individual poem are from the poems of Edward Taylor (Yale University Press, 1963: Donald E. Sanford, editor). Taylor and Sewall were bunk-mates at Harvard.

Two of the individual poems (XII and XV), appeared in slightly different versions, in *Kennebec*, published at the University of Maine at Augusta.

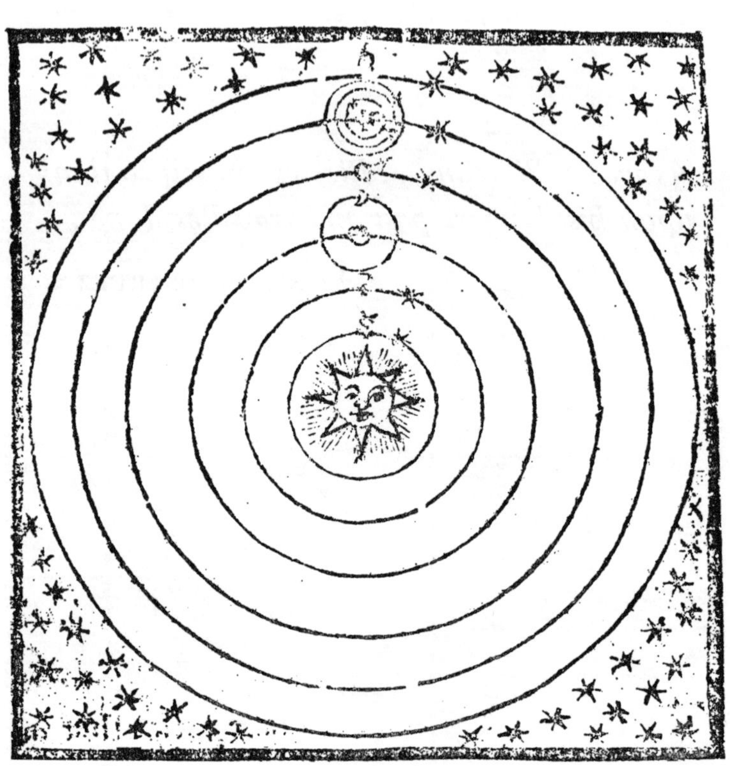

I
April, 1674

I'm sick: my sickness is mortality . . .

Benjamin Gourd, age seventeen,
having for a year or more lived in
this abominable, filthy Sin,
in open noonday yard was seen
consorting with a roan mare.
This day, for bestiality,
Benjamin Gourd, bound tightly,
comes to the gallows tree. There
the Mare was brought and struck down
screaming in the mud before his eyes.
Would he wake before he drowns?
Would he take to Paradise
or Hell this vision of great brown
orbs fixed forever on the ground?

II

The First Dream: July, 1675

*I shall rise in Glories Dress to meet thee
in the skies.*

With dead child in arms I mount
an endless stair. The mother follows
weeping, wailing out her sorrow.
Steps sweep up—I can not count
them—still no Heaven. Still no rest.
No *sedes beatorum*. We struggle upward.
With shame I weaken. Afterward
I marvel how adversity contests
faith. We reach a timbered room. High,
goodly lodging, but earth-bound
stuff: tables, chairs, sideboards, chests. My
dazed fancy, on waking, found
no clue. Solid timbers in the sky.
How are they lifted up so high?

III

The Second Dream: June, 1685

My Love alas is but a shrimpy thing . . .

Too sweet, too soon, first of June
day, for sweating heat or dust.
Riding down from Newbury just
at dusk to find black plumes
smothering all joy of home.
Hannah, ten years my wife, dead!
My shouts echo as if my head's
an empty grave. *Hannah, I'm home!*
Mother's gone neglected to her tomb,
my daughter says. Oh tortured rest!
Oh morning bring release from doom!
At blessed waking Hannah's at my breast
as if fresh from the Bridal Room.
(. . . *quasi nuper nuptam amplexus sum!*)

IV

The Third Dream: Jan., 1685/6

The Word-Made-Flesh. Here's Grace's 'mazing stride.

How blessed our city on the hill.
Higher than Rome our Zion sits,
their Peter by our Savior eclipsed!
In His days of flesh His will
brought our Lord to Boston; more
to my wonder, at Father Hull's
takes lodging. How the familiar dulls
my sense. To my Hannah's door
Jesus turns, and with him comes
more honor to my earthly father.
Thus I recognize the sum
of his virtues. And our Father
adds this to His glory, to come
as we have, to New Jerusalem.

V

Cold Christmas: Dec., 1687

Eate, Eate me, Soul, and thou shalt never dy.

The Indian, Henry, frozen white,
lost while crossing the river
on the ice. Carters delivering
firewood find him at first light.
Sleds come, shops open, as on any
day. No Papist celebration seen.
A new snow sweeps each street clean
of tracks. There'll not be as many
gone to worship as yesterday
when the frozen sacramental bread
broken in the plate, rattled sadly.
But the Sun will keep its head,
come back slow and sure each day.
Birds again will have their say.

VI

The Fourth Dream: Dec., 1688

A sea of Liquid Gold with rocks of Pearle . . .

Wind North North-West. Storms of hail,
flaws, assault our ship. But soon
decks dry. In the afternoon
sun breaks astern and we sail
toward but never reach the rainbow.
As in my dream my wife holds out
a piece of cake, but bound about,
I can not reach her. Now below
me she's brought to bed with child
while I'm somehow trapped above
the highest gallery. When the child
cries out, I can not show my love.
Storm waves batter all the while.
I'm wet, retching, choked on bile.

VII

The Fifth Dream: Dec., 1688

Hell's Scarlet Dy fat, blood red grown with Sin.

Last night I dreamed of military
matters: Captains, arms — but suddenly
a shape appears with lively
countenance, blood-red finery.
In silken breeches, a silken coat,
Major Gookin, smiling, calls me,
beckons me to follow. I see
his soft face in scarlet cloak afloat.
I grip the bed rails as if
it were my soul he'd tear
from me. When I wake all stiff,
cold, I remember the garret stairs.
Oakes dreamed Mitchell would lure him there.
I shudder in the ship's dank air.

VIII

The Court Sits in Salem: June, 1692

Sin Craks the Axle tree of this Great Cart.

At Salem Meeting House so pressed
the crowd we scarce cleared a place
for Judges, afflicted, accused, to face
Justice and each other. I'm distressed
beyond forgetting to see victims
stagger, gasp for breath, shriek, fall
twitching in the dust. And I recall
a dream forgotten, an omen.
Father Hull burying . . . I can't see
who. Heard him say, *Now it seems
we go to Salem!* — this being
how proper time is bent by dreams.
So we set about the freeing
of Souls: send the Devil fleeing.

IX

The Sixth Dream: Jan., 1694/5

My tazzled Thoughts twirled into Snick-Snarls run . . .

How was it I knew of it?
How could the father succeed
the son? Mr. Adams too felt need
to come . . . Where Oakes, the father, sits
before us as he had in life.
Again chosen Pastor to
Cambridge Church. His ruddy hue
fresh as a child's, yet the knife
of time cut him sharply down
years ago. His son followed after.
What Spirits draw a mist around
my mind? Among shadowed rafters
above my bed the Devil clowns,
spins this blind man round, around.

X

The Seventh Dream: March, 1694/5

The Dove must die. The storm gives up its ghost.

Jane, Judith, Stephen, Henry, Hull,
John, all gone. Last night it seemed
all but baby Sarah had now streamed
after to the swelling tomb. How dull
was the balance of our life
to be if Samuel, little Hannah,
Betty, Joseph, Mary, all the manna
of nineteen years of wifely
travail, were also called to Heaven.
This was a vision to remember
when Sarah joined those seven
kittens suckling at the cold, December
breast of death. Thus do dreams leaven
fear: but prayers do rise to Heaven.

XI
Repentance: Dec.-Jan., 1696 / 7

Guilty, my Lord, What can I more declare?
Thou Knowest the Case . . .

One cold, gray day marked Christ's birth,
and the burial of that small sprite
of flesh, Sarah. Samuel recites.
We Pray. At Matthew 12 my earth
shook: "*. . . if ye had known what this*
meaneth" (can this sinner make amends?)
"*ye would not have condemned*
the guiltless." Thus, as weak tears kissed
her cold face, my resolve began.
Now, before God, I stand to hear
my words read: how my zeal outran
evidence. Of Salem's trial — I fear
the Blame and Shame of it. Ban
us not, Lord, for one weak man.

XII

To Mrs. Martha Oakes: Sept., 1696

Words . . . written only inked paper bee.

Madam, I write to persuade you
to be sensible: for New England
is a cleaner country than
ever you were in before. To
disdain it filthy is a sort
of Blasphemy which, as proceeds
from your mouth, must needs
defile you. I write this not
to upbraid, but only to advise
you and pray God commands you
to see the truth and your eyes
should show you, your heart know, true
joy in what you would despise.
Know us, Lady, let your spirit rise.

XIII

Ezekiel Chiever, Dying: Aug., 1708

Lord blow the Coal: Thy Love Enflame in mee.

Mr. Chiever, dying, I sit with him
again. Yesterday he roused to say,
*Afflictions of God's people may
be as the Goldsmith, to trim
to finish the plate. Knock, knock,
knock, knock, knock: to perfect,
not punish them.* He expects
me to pray, Mr. Williams not
coming when called. He meekly
sucks the Orange that I brought
despite the Cancer has nearly
burned one jaw away. He caught
the pulp with his hand neatly,
signed he heard me; wept most sweetly.

XIV

Treaty Conference at Arrowsick: Aug., 1717

Words spoken are but breezing boxed winde.

Savages resplendent in their paint:
are they God's sons, their distance
from us a film of circumstance
as thin as water's, where my faint
image twists in monstrous shapes,
where cast-off cockle shells become
now sharp, now rheumy: the one
no truer than the other? Truth escapes
again, but we must set right
bounds against the Frenchman's rage.
Beauty burns about us day and night.
We see but trees where Savages
do the Devil's work and ever fight
our Lord with horrid arrow's flight.

XV

On the Kennebec: Aug., 1717

And in God's Garden saw a Golden Tree.

Becalmed. I go ashore on
the Small Point side. A settlement,
rotted down, had signed its intent
with apple trees. All buildings gone.
Loon birds, silent, dive to meet
the flooding tide. All about me
faithful, abandoned, fruitful trees
abide. Twisted brier, berries, defeat
each other as they fight to rise.
Lost apples fruitful still—Praised be!
Man, and not the tree, denies
Paradise. A butterfly slowly
unfolds. From rank leaves passion flies,
a greedy, gorging worm surprised.

XVI

His Convent: Aug., 1728

. . . nimble Flashes dancing on each thing . . .

His bright omen, the rainbow, rises
from Dorchester Neck to span
the Town. Hard cracks of thunder ran
before it. Lightning, sharp, surprises
souls unwilling. In fresh washed air
Swallows from the eaves are filled
with empty, happy chatter. Distilled
by sun, raindrops rise, flare,
weight the air with earthy scents.
Such things move among days heavy
with funerals of old friends. Bent
backs are fit bearers as Time levies
tax on our inheritance.
Earth, newborn, moves on intent.

XVII

A Last Dream: Sept., 1728

The Painter lies who pensills death's Face grim.

It was a common, ragged boy
stole time. Not gaunt death who ran,
silver flashing in his hand.
He tossed my watch up as a toy.
He could not read my distich.
Five of my own children learned
this rhyme, in simple Latin, turned
about the silver case as seconds ticked
away. *As long as ear, mind,*
eye, hand, bone, foot, still carry on
it's more important that we find
truth than stay a fool. Whereon
I gave the boy a second watch for mine,
which now, in morning's window, shines.

XVIII

Sailing for Home: Jan. 1, 1729/30

The Grave's a Down bed now made for your clay.

My bed lifts up on oily waves
as if cast adrift upon the bay,
pitching, yawing—this way, that way—
I clutch the coverlet to save
myself. Now my Joseph's face
(Holy vessel) swimming up
into my view (Blessed cup)
filled forever with her grace.
As wavering reflections by his side,
Hannah and her sleeping children
hold out hungry arms. I slide
toward them with leaden
limbs as sea-wrack on ebb tide
returns to sea. What will abide?

This edition of Samuel Sewall Sails for Home *consists of 500 copies, composed in Linotype Janson and printed at the Anthoensen Press, Portland, Maine.*